SURVIVAL GUIDE

The Perfect Five

Ralph McCall

Think Deep! Series

destinēe

COPYRIGHT

Survival Guide, The Perfect Five: Think Deep!
By Ralph McCall

© Copyright 2025 by Ralph McCall

All rights reserved. No part of this publication may be reproduced, distributed, or transmitted in any form or by any means, including photocopying, recording, or other electronic or mechanical methods, without the prior written permission of the publisher, except in the case of brief quotations embodied in critical reviews and specific other noncommercial uses permitted by copyright law.

Scripture quotations marked (NIV) are taken from the Holy Bible, New International Version®, NIV®. Copyright © 1973, 1978, 1984, 2011 by Biblica, Inc.™ Used by permission. All rights reserved worldwide.

Scripture quotations marked (ESV) are from the ESV® Bible (The Holy Bible, English Standard Version®), Copyright © 2001 by Crossway, a publishing ministry of Good News Publishers. Used by permission. All rights reserved.

Scripture quotations marked (NLT) are taken from the Holy Bible, New Living Translation, Copyright © 1996, 2004, 2015 by Tyndale House Foundation. Used by permission. All rights reserved.

Published by Destinee Media, www.destineemedia.com
Written by Ralph McCall

ISBN: 978-1938367908

CONTENTS

Copyright ii
Contents iii
Think Deep! Series iv
Introduction 1
Chapter 1: Solus Christus – Only Christ 6
Chapter 2: Sola Scriptura – Only Scripture 14
Chapter 3: Sola Gratia – Only Grace 23
Chapter 4: Sola Fide – Only Faith 31
Chapter 5: Soli Deo Gloria – Only to the glory of God 39
Finally: Anchored in the Five Solas for Our Age 49

THINK DEEP! SERIES

Survival Guide: The Perfect Five is part of the **Think Deep! Series**, created for those who want more than surface answers.

Each book in the series explores the big questions about culture, identity, and faith—designed for a digital generation immersed in an endless array of perspectives and ever-shifting narratives.

To develop true and just discernment.

INTRODUCTION

The Five Solas – Survival Guide Foundations in a Fragmented Age

---

When Everything Feels Uncertain

Open TikTok, Instagram, or YouTube, and your feed flips in seconds. One minute you're inspired. The next, you're overwhelmed. One day, your identity is a personality type or a trend. The next, it's something totally new. It's easy to feel like truth is just... whatever's popular that week.

Even in some churches, the message sounds more like life coaching or social commentary. And deep down, you might wonder:
Where's the truth that actually holds up?
Where's something solid I can build my life on?

That's where five short Latin phrases come in—not as dusty theology, but as *anchors*:

- **Solus Christus** – *Only Christ*
- **Sola Scriptura** – *Only Scripture*
- **Sola Gratia** – *Only Grace*
- **Sola Fide** – *Only Faith*
- **Soli Deo Gloria** – *Only to the glory of God*

At first, they might sound ancient. But these truths are more relevant now than ever. When your world feels like a million puzzle pieces that won't fit together, the *solas* show you how the gospel holds it all.

Back in the 1500s, a group of believers known as the **Reformers** discovered these truths again. They weren't just trying to fix a broken church—they were uncovering the *heart of the gospel*. As Martin Luther put it:

"My conscience is captive to the Word of God."

He wasn't saying, "Let's tear everything down."
He was saying, *"Let's go back to what's real. To God's voice. To Christ's work. To grace you don't have to earn."*

We need that same return today.

By The Way—Martin Luther wasn't just a name in your history class. He was a monk in Germany who had a major "wait a second" moment with the Church.

Back then, people were told they could *pay* their way into heaven or earn it through rituals. Luther read the Bible and realized: **salvation comes by faith, not good behavior or money.** In 1517, he nailed 95 of his thoughts to a church door—and let's say, the church leaders were *not* thrilled.

His ideas kicked off a movement that reshaped Christianity and still affects how we follow Jesus today—even if we don't always talk about him.

You'll see a few of his quotes in this book, along with wisdom from other solid Bible thinkers.

The Gospel vs. a Culture of Deconstruction

Back then, they challenged a corrupt church.
Today, you face something different: a world that says *nothing is really true.*
You've probably heard it:

- "Everyone has their own truth."
- "Just follow your heart."
- "Do what feels right to you."

And if you've ever felt confused, or cynical, or spiritually numb—you're not alone.

A philosopher named Jacques Derrida once said, *"There is nothing outside the text."* It sounds abstract, but it shaped a mindset that's everywhere now:
Words mean whatever you want.
Truth is fluid.
Morality? Pick your version.

But here's the problem:
That freedom often leads to *anxiety*, *exhaustion*, and *loneliness*.

The five solas speak back—with clarity and hope:

- **Solus Christus**: In a sea of options, *Jesus* is the one steady anchor.
- **Sola Scriptura**: Truth isn't something you invent—it's something God *reveals*.
- **Sola Gratia**: You don't have to earn love or fix yourself—*grace does the work*.
- **Sola Fide**: You're not defined by hustle or likes—you're made right through *faith*.
- **Soli Deo Gloria**: Life isn't ultimately about *you*—it's about reflecting *God's glory*.

These solas don't whisper—they **shout**.
They re-center your faith when everything around you spins.
They bring you back to God's unshakable love.

Speaking Truth Into the Cultural Noise

This isn't just a church issue—it's everywhere.
You're swimming in messages that sound spiritual but quietly pull you away from God.

Let's name a few:

Expressive Individualism

"Be true to yourself."
→ **Soli Deo Gloria** reminds you: *You were made to reflect God—not just follow your feelings.*

Therapeutic Spirituality

"Find peace and good vibes."
→ **Sola Gratia** says: *Grace isn't surface-level—it changes your heart from the inside out.*

Technocratic Optimism

"Tech will fix everything."
→ **Solus Christus** says: *No app, no AI, no breakthrough can replace what only Jesus can do.*

Identity Politics

"My label is my truth."
→ **Soli Deo Gloria** says: *You are more than a category—you were made to display God's worth.*

These trends promise freedom, but often leave us anxious, divided, and exhausted.

The Five Solas offer something far better:

- **Peace** instead of pressure
- **Truth** instead of confusion
- **Rest** instead of hustle
- **God's love** instead of fear

A Blueprint for Renewal

This isn't just a theology book—it's **a survival guide for your soul**.

Every chapter will:

- Break down one sola in plain, relatable language
- Show how it's rooted in Scripture
- Compare it to today's cultural messages
- Help you live it out in real life: your friendships, your faith, even your screen time

Each sola is a thread—and together, they weave a clear picture of **Jesus, His gospel, and your purpose in His story**.

These aren't just truths from the past.
They're how we resist the lies around us today.
They're how we recover what it means to be fully alive in God.

What's Next: *Solus Christus* – Only Christ

In a world where everyone wants to make their own truth, the idea that only Jesus is *the* way can feel either offensive… or like the *first breath of real hope*.

Jesus isn't another voice in the algorithm.
He's the One who knows your name.
He doesn't ask you to impress Him—He invites you to *trust Him*.

In the next chapter, we'll explore **Solus Christus** and how Jesus isn't just a way—He's *the Way*. He meets your deepest need—not with hype, but with *grace*, *truth*, and *resurrection power*.

When everything else fails, **Only Christ remains**.

CHAPTER 1: SOLUS CHRISTUS – ONLY CHRIST

Why Only Jesus Still Offends—and Saves—in an Age of Spiritual Options

---

What If There's Only One Way—Not Many?

Have you ever wondered why, in a world that celebrates endless options, the name *Jesus* still makes people uncomfortable?

You can talk about spirituality, energy, or "the universe"—no problem. But mention Jesus as the only way to God, and suddenly the air changes. People shift. Eyes drop. Some get angry. Some walk away.

Why?

Because saying *Only Christ* cuts through the noise. It doesn't flatter us. It doesn't give us control. It calls us to surrender—to trust someone outside of ourselves.

But here's the twist: it also speaks the deepest kind of love.

This message isn't about being superior. It's about finding fulfillment, not by climbing to God, but by God coming for you.

In today's world, we have so many choices—about who we are, what we believe, and how we find meaning. Everyone has "their own truth." So when someone says **Jesus is the only way**, it can feel narrow. But this message is not about being better than others. It's about the deep, beautiful truth of **God's love for you**.

Martin Luther once said,

"The cross alone is our theology."

He meant that the **heart of Christianity** is not about church rules, trying hard, or being spiritual enough. It's about **Jesus**, who died and rose again to bring you to God.

John Calvin warned that our hearts are like **idol factories**—we often build new ways to feel good or spiritual without Christ. Today, those idols include:

- **Relativism**: "Your truth" and "my truth."
- **Deconstruction**: Taking faith apart but never rebuilding it.
- **Me-centered spirituality**: Making yourself the center of the story.
- **Experiential religion**: Ginn up your emotions in a religious setting and a spirit manifests. But what spirit?

But *Solus Christus*—**Only Christ**—reminds us:
Jesus is not one option. He is the only one who saves.

Besides Luther, here's another person. John Calvin was a historical guy who lived during the time of Luther, and he came to the same conclusions as Luther. You can't do works to gain favor with God.

Way back in 1536, Calvin published a book titled *Institutes of the Christian Religion*. It had a huge influence back then, and his ideas carry on today. It just shows you that old thoughts based on truth are timeless. Calvin will be quoted in this book.

What Does *Solus Christus* Mean?

1. The Heart of the Message

Solus Christus means **Only Christ**. It says clearly:
No other person, ritual, or good work can save us. Only Jesus can.

"For there is one God, and there is one mediator between God and men, the man Christ Jesus."

— 1 Timothy 2:5 (ESV)

Here are **three powerful truths** behind that:

1. **Jesus is both fully God and fully human.**
2. **His sacrifice on the cross is enough.** He paid for your sins completely.
3. **Nothing else needs to be added.** Not saints, not rituals, not personal effort.

---

2. Rooted in the Bible

Jesus says clearly:

"I am the way, and the truth, and the life. No one comes to the Father except through me."
— John 14:6 (ESV)

Peter confirms it:

"There is salvation in no one else, for there is no other name under heaven given among men by which we must be saved."
— Acts 4:12 (ESV)

We live in a time where a lot of people are searching for something more—some kind of deep spiritual experience. Some look for it in meditation, success, or personal growth. Others try to find secret shortcuts to heaven. But Jesus already told us the truth.

"I am the door. If anyone enters by Me, he will be saved." — John 10:9 (ESV)

Jesus doesn't say *He's one of many doors.* He says He's **the door**.

This is both **inclusive** and **exclusive**.
It's *inclusive* because **anyone** can come to Him—no matter your past, your background, or your struggles.
It's *exclusive* because **Jesus is the only way**.

In another place, Jesus says something equally as powerful:

"These are the words of him who is holy and true, who holds the key of David. What he opens no one can shut, and what he shuts no one can open." — Revelation 3:7 (ESV)

Jesus holds the **key**. This means He has **full authority**—He is the one who opens the door to heaven. And once He opens it for you, no one can shut it.

Let's make it simple with a picture:

Imagine you're stuck in a giant maze. You try every hallway, every turn, but all of them lead to dead ends.
Then, finally, you see a single door—and that door leads to freedom, peace, and purpose.
That door is **Jesus**, and He holds the **only key** that fits.

So here's the good news:
You don't need to keep searching.
You don't need to try a million paths.
Jesus is the way to God.
And He's already inviting you in.

---

3. It Changed History

Before the Reformation, people believed they needed to go through priests, rituals, and rules to get to heaven. And give money. You had to do religious "works" to reach God. (Unfortunately, we find the same thing today.)

But in *The Babylonian Captivity of the Church* (1520), Luther boldly said: You don't need anyone between you and God. **You can go directly to Him.**

That idea was revolutionary.

Historian D. Blair Smith writes:
"Solus Christus drove the whole program of reform… scrubbing away the pollution of man-made tradition."

It's an incredible privilege to have Jesus as your Savior. It means you can speak to God at any time and from any place. And he always listens. This communication is called **prayer**.

Why "Only Christ" Still Matters Today

1. If We Lose This, We Lose Everything

Without Only Christ:

- The **cross becomes pointless**.
- Jesus becomes **just another helper**, not the Savior.
- Grace feels like something we must **earn** instead of **receive**.

But the Bible says:

"The righteousness of God through faith in Jesus Christ for all who believe. For there is no distinction."
— Romans 3:22 (ESV)

"For our sake he made him to be sin who knew no sin, so that in him we might become the righteousness of God."
— 2 Corinthians 5:21 (ESV)

"So Christ, having been offered once to bear the sins of many, will appear a second time… to save those who are eagerly waiting for him."
— Hebrews 9:28 (ESV)

You don't have to wonder if you're good enough. **Jesus already was.**

2. What It Means for You

Solus Christus is not just a church word. It's **personal**.

- **Peace**: You don't need to be perfect. Jesus gives it.
- **Worship**: Church is not about performance and emotional highs—it's about loving Jesus.
- **Identity**: You are more than your past, your labels, or your failures. You are loved and made new in Christ.

Martin Luther said:
"The gospel tells me not what I must do, but what Jesus Christ... has done for me."

Who Is Jesus, Really?

Let's look at what the Bible says in **Colossians 1**:

"He is the image of the invisible God... all things were created through him and for him... He is before all things, and in him all things hold together."
— Colossians 1:15–20 (ESV)

What This Means:

1. **Jesus shows us who God is.**
2. **He created everything—** even you.
3. **He holds your life together, even when it feels like it's falling apart.**
4. **He gives new life to His people.**
5. **Through Jesus, we have peace with God.**

Christ vs. Today's Culture

Culture says:

- "Make your own truth."
- "Do what feels right."
- "Just believe in yourself."

But Jesus says:

- "I am the truth."
- "Follow me."
- "You don't have to save yourself—I already did."

Michael Kruger writes:
"*Solus Christus* fights against pluralism—the idea that all religious pathways are valid."

No Add-Ons, Upgrades. No Downgrades.

Do we need to add rituals or extra rules to Jesus?

Do we need to reduce Him to just a wise teacher, social helper, or way-shower?

In a world full of upgrades and customizations, Jesus stays the same. He is **complete**, just as He is.

"He is the image of the invisible God… making peace by the blood of his cross."
— Colossians 1:15, 19–20 (ESV)
"Jesus Christ is the same yesterday and today and forever."
— Hebrews 13:8 (ESV)

With Jesus, there are no upgrades or downgrades. He is God.

Final Thoughts: What Does "Only Christ" Mean for You?

This isn't about being religious. It's about being **loved by God** through Jesus.

When you believe in Only Christ:

- You are **fully forgiven**.
- You can **talk to God anytime**.
- You are not alone—Jesus walks with you.

"Jesus said to him, 'I am the way, and the truth, and the life. No one comes to the Father except through me.'"
— John 14:6 (ESV)

No one else will do.

No one else is needed.

Only Christ—always.

What's Next: Solus Scriptura – Only Scripture

In the next chapter, we'll explore *Solus Scriptura* and how God has given you the ultimate guide for navigating life. It's like having a GPS for your soul—showing you where to go, what matters most, and how to stay grounded in a world that's constantly shifting.

CHAPTER 2: SOLA SCRIPTURA – ONLY SCRIPTURE

"God's Word Alone: The Final Authority in a World of Competing Voices"

Scripture is like having the ultimate GPS—but for your whole life. It shows you where you are, tells you what's real and true around you, and leads you in the right direction—no matter how lost the world feels.

Why "Only Scripture" Still Matters Today

We live in a time that feels like shifting sand. One day, something is "right." The next day, it's canceled. Everyone seems to be shouting:

- "Truth is whatever *you* feel!"
- "You do *you*!"
- "There's no right or wrong—just *your* truth and *my* truth."

This is called **Postmodernism**. It's the idea that **truth is personal, not universal**. In this kind of culture, people often choose their feelings or preferences over facts. Even **God's Word** can be pushed aside.

But the Bible gently says something very different:

"The grass withers, the flower fades, but the word of our God will stand forever." — Isaiah 40:8 (ESV)

In a world where everything feels temporary and unstable, God offers us **a steady anchor—His Word.**

That's the heart of *Sola Scriptura*—**Only Scripture**.
It means: **Only the Bible is perfect, eternal, and has the final say.**

What *Sola Scriptura* Means

"Sola Scriptura" is a Latin phrase that means "Only Scripture." It's not against learning from teachers, traditions, or feelings. But it means **everything else must sit below God's Word—not above it.**

John Frame explains,
"Sola Scriptura means that our ultimate authority is the Bible—and nothing else."

Jesus prayed to the Father:

"Sanctify them through thy truth: thy word is truth." — John 17:17 (KJV)

This is personal. **God's Word changes you.** It's not just information—it's transformation.

As you open the Bible, God speaks—not just to the world, but **to your heart.**

Scripture's Promises

The Bible says so much about its own beauty and power:

"All Scripture is breathed out by God and profitable... that the man of God may be complete, equipped for every good work." — 2 Timothy 3:16–17 (ESV)

"Man shall not live by bread alone, but by every word that comes from the mouth of God." — Matthew 4:4 (ESV)

"The law of the Lord is perfect, reviving the soul... the commandment of the Lord is pure, enlightening the eyes." — Psalm 19:7–9 (ESV)

God's Word revives, corrects, feeds, and fills. No social media post, no trending opinion, no celebrity advice can match that.

How the Church Lost—and Found—This Truth

By the 1500s, many church leaders had placed tradition, rituals, and human authority **above** the Bible. They taught that people couldn't fully understand Scripture without a priest.

The Reformers, like **Martin Luther** and **John Calvin**, were bold enough to say:

"My conscience is captive to the Word of God." — Martin Luther
"The Word of God is the foundation of all true religion." — John Calvin

They didn't want something new. They wanted to **return** to God's voice in the Bible.

Creeds like the **Westminster Confession** and the **Belgic Confession** followed their lead, teaching that *Only Scripture* is the "only rule for faith and life."

Voices that Still Echo

Even in recent years, Christian teachers remind us that Scripture is still central:

- **R.C. Sproul**: *"Where Scripture speaks, God speaks."*
- **John MacArthur**: *"If you want to hear God speak, read the Bible out loud."*
- **Alistair Begg**: *"The Bible is a rock in a sea of confusion."*
- **John Piper**: *"The Bible is the voice of God, and it has final authority."*
- **Kevin DeYoung**: *"Scripture is enough because the work of Christ is enough. They stand or fall together."*
- **Michael Horton**: *"To deny the sufficiency of Scripture is to deny the sufficiency of Christ."*

These guys have done their homework, and these quotes aren't just smart—they're **lifelines** in a confused world.

The Spirit Who Illuminates the Word

Sola Scriptura teaches us that the Bible is God's final and full message to us. But that raises an important question: **How do we actually understand what the Bible says?**

The answer is simple: **first, the Holy Spirit.**

But what's that exactly?

The Holy Spirit is **fully God**—the third Person of the Trinity—**equal with the Father and the Son**. Just as the **Father speaks** and the **Son is the Living Word**, the **Spirit gives life and understanding.**

The Holy Spirit is not just a vague feeling or inner energy.

The same God who inspired the Bible also makes it clear and powerful to us.

Jesus promised this very thing when He said:

"When the Spirit of truth comes, he will guide you into all the truth..." — John 16:13 (ESV)

The Spirit doesn't add new revelations. He doesn't give us private truth or secret messages. Instead, **He helps us truly see and trust the truth that's already in Scripture.** This isn't guesswork or emotion—it's divine light.

Paul explains how this happens:

"Now we have received not the spirit of the world, but the Spirit who is from God, that we might understand the things freely given us by God." — 1 Corinthians 2:12 (ESV)

"The natural person does not accept the things of the Spirit of God... and he is not able to understand them because they are spiritually discerned." — 1 Corinthians 2:14 (ESV)

In other words, these verses remind us: **we <u>need</u> the Holy Spirit to open our eyes.**

Even though the Bible is clear, our hearts can be hard or distracted. That's why Paul prays for believers like this:

"...that the God of our Lord Jesus Christ, the Father of glory, may give you the Spirit of wisdom and of revelation in the knowledge of him, having the eyes of your hearts enlightened..." — Ephesians 1:17–18 (ESV)

Reading the Bible isn't just an academic exercise. It's an **act of worship.**
We depend on the **same Spirit who hovered over the waters in Genesis,** bringing order out of chaos. He still brings:

- **Light** to places that feel dark
- **Clarity** when we feel confused
- **A gentle push** when we want to resist

So when we say "Sola Scriptura," we're not saying "me and my Bible alone."
We're saying:
"God's Word is my authority—and I trust the Spirit to help me receive it."

This is why we read the Bible prayerfully.
This is why we listen carefully.
Because the Spirit is present—**fully God, fully powerful, fully gracious**—**revealing Christ to us through the Word.**

But How Do We *Understand* the Bible?

Let's be real—some people open the Bible and treat it like a mystery code or a personal journal that says whatever they feel. But the Bible isn't a puzzle or a mood ring.

God speaks clearly. And He wants to be understood.

So how do we read it the right way? One proven method is called the **historical-grammatical-literal** approach. That sounds complicated—but it's actually simple:

- **Historical**: What did it mean to the people back then? What was going on in their world?
- **Grammatical**: What do the words and sentences really say? (Yes—grammar matters!)
- **Literal**: Read it as the author meant it—poetry as poetry, stories as stories, commands as commands.

This method helps us **let Scripture explain itself**—instead of twisting it into whatever we want it to mean.

It's not about being cold or technical. It's about **respecting God's words**, not rewriting them. When we read the Bible this way, it becomes clear, powerful, and deeply personal—without becoming self-centered.

The result? You hear what *God* is actually saying. Not just your own echo.

What Postmodern Culture Gets Wrong

Today's culture often says:

- "Truth is whatever you feel."
- "No one can tell you what's right or wrong."
- "Your identity is what you decide."

But these ideas are exhausting. They promise freedom but give confusion.

Sola Scriptura says:

Truth is not something we create.
It's something we **receive** from a loving, holy, and unchanging God.

Where Culture Collides with God's Word

Let's be honest. There's a battle going on inside and around us:

God's Word Says	Postmodern Culture Says
Truth is objective and eternal	Truth is personal and shifting
God defines who we are	You define yourself
Submit to God's authority	Live for yourself
Scripture tells us what is right or wrong	Morality depends on the situation or emotion

The result? If we follow the culture, we lose our foundation. But if we follow Scripture, we find peace, clarity, and purpose.

Without Scripture, We Drift

When the church forgets God's Word:

- Truth turns into opinion
- Confidence becomes shaky
- Unity turns into division

But when we come back to **Sola Scriptura**:

- We know who God is
- We know who we are
- We know what is true

God is not hiding. He is speaking—**through His Word.**

Anchored in the Voice of Christ

Let's remember these truths:

- **The Bible is our final authority**
- **Its truth comes from God, not man**
- **It guards the gospel and shapes real life**
- **It pushes back against confusion and lies**

"Scripture is enough because the work of Christ is enough." — Kevin DeYoung
"Where Scripture speaks, God speaks." — R.C. Sproul

We don't worship the Bible—we worship **the God who speaks through it.**
When you open the Bible, it's not just a page—it's a doorway to knowing Jesus.

A Gentle Challenge

Let the Bible be your compass:

- **Read it every day**—even a few verses
- **Ask the Holy Spirit to help**
- **Let God's voice be louder than your feelings**
- **Let His truth shape how you see the world—and yourself**

Jesus prayed,
"Sanctify them in the truth; your word is truth." — John 17:17 (ESV)

What's Next: Sola Gratia – Only Grace

Now that we know **where truth comes from**, we'll discover **how grace saves us.**

It's not about earning. It's about receiving. And **the Bible will show us how.**

Stay close to the Word—because that's where you'll find the heart of Jesus.

CHAPTER 3: SOLA GRATIA – ONLY GRACE

The Unmerited Favor That Saves the Undeserving

Introduction: The Fountainhead of Redemption

Many people today no longer talk about *sin*. In classrooms, on the news, and in our social feeds, we hear about "mistakes," "trauma," and "self-acceptance." Pain is often explained away as emotional imbalance or bad choices. Right and wrong become matters of opinion. The word *sin* sounds outdated—even offensive.

But when we lose the language of sin, we also lose the hope of grace.

If we don't know we're lost, why would we ever look for rescue? Without understanding our sin, the cross seems unnecessary. We turn to therapy, self-help, or self-improvement—but these cannot touch the soul-deep guilt and brokenness we carry. We remain cut off from God, aching for healing we cannot produce.

Yet into this hopelessness, God speaks one word that changes everything: **grace**.

Grace is not God helping the strong get stronger. It is not a gentle push for good people trying hard. Grace is the wild, undeserved, astonishing love of God for the unworthy, the broken, and the dead. It is *God coming all the way down*—to lift us up.

"And you were dead in the trespasses and sins in which you once walked... But God, being rich in mercy, because of the great love with which he loved us... made us alive together with Christ—by grace you have been saved."
— *Ephesians 2:1, 4–5 (ESV)*

"While we were still weak... Christ died for the ungodly... God shows his love for us in that while we were still sinners, Christ died for us."
— *Romans 5:6, 8 (ESV)*

John Calvin once said:

"Grace does not find men fit to be saved, but makes them so."

In a world driven by achievement, self-worth, and performance, **Sola Gratia**—Only Grace—can sound scandalous. It tells us that we cannot earn God's favor. We are not saved because of who we are, but in spite of who we are. Grace humbles the proud—and heals the hopeless.

As J. I. Packer wrote:

"Grace is the heart of the Christian faith; without it, all else is dead formalism."

Sola Gratia whispers into every heart:

You are more sinful than you ever feared—but more loved than you ever dreamed.

From eternity past to eternity future, salvation is entirely God's gift to the undeserving. And it flows not from our effort, but from His everlasting love.

Defining *Sola Gratia*

"By grace we mean that unconditional favor of God granted to undeserving sinners for their regeneration and sanctification."
— *Wayne Grudem, Systematic Theology*

- **Sola** (Latin): alone, only
- **Gratia** (Latin): grace, undeserved favor

Sola Gratia means that our salvation—beginning to end—is entirely the work of God's free and loving choice. Nothing in us can make us worthy of it. No effort or religious act can earn it. Even the very faith we use to receive grace is a gift.

"By the grace of God I am what I am, and his grace toward me was not in vain."
— *1 Corinthians 15:10 (ESV)*

Grace is not cold doctrine—it's God's warm, pursuing love. It finds us when we've run too far. It reaches us when we've sunk too deep. It restores us when we are too weak to lift our heads.

Grace is the free gift from God through the sacrifice of Christ on the cross. When we realize our rebellion and separation from Him, and when we accept that gift of Grace, God makes us perfect and pure in His sight. And you have an eternal relationship with him.

That's right. It's a **free gift from God**.

The Biblical Foundation

The Bible is not vague about grace—it shouts it from beginning to end:

"For by grace you have been saved through faith. And this is not your own doing; it is the gift of God…" *Ephesians 2:1–10*

We were spiritually dead, but God made us alive.

"While we were still weak… Christ died for the ungodly." *Romans 5:6–11*

Christ didn't wait for us to clean up—He died for us while we were still sinners.

"If it is by grace, it is no longer on the basis of works; otherwise, grace would no longer be grace." *Romans 11:5–6*

Every word echoes the same truth:
Grace is not God's response to our goodness—it is His answer to our need.

The Reformation Recovery of Grace

As stated before, by the 1500s, the Church had begun to trade grace for human effort. It taught that salvation came through religious performance—penance, indulgences, sacraments. Grace was still mentioned, but only as something we *add to* with our deeds.

The Reformers recovered what had been lost: the shocking, humbling, freeing truth that **salvation is all of grace**.

- **Martin Luther** found peace at last in the book of Romans. With this understanding, he taught that we are justified by grace through faith alone—not by climbing a spiritual ladder.

- **John Calvin** emphasized that grace is sovereign and effective by saying, "God draws those whom He has chosen, and makes them willing."

The great Reformation confessions—**Augsburg**, **Westminster**, **Dort**—made *Sola Gratia* a foundation stone of the gospel. Grace is not one ingredient in salvation. It is the cause behind it all.

The Biblical Argument for Sola Gratia

Theological Necessity

1. **Total Depravity Requires Total Grace**
   We are not spiritually sick—we are spiritually dead (Eph. 2:1). We do not seek God (Rom. 3:11). If God did not come to us, we would never go to Him.

2. **Grace Must Be Sovereign, Not Solicited**
   Grace that waits for us to act first is no longer grace.

   > "So then it depends not on human will or exertion, but on God, who has mercy." — *Romans 9:16*

   > "Grace is never earned. It is God's favor despite who we are." — *D. A. Carson*

3. **Grace Is the Source of Faith**
   Even our faith is God's gift.

   > "It has been granted to you… that you should believe…" — *Philippians 1:29*

Common Misunderstandings

Some people think that grace means we no longer have to care about doing good. But that's not it. Grace doesn't cancel good works—it powers them. You're not working *for* salvation; you're working *from* salvation. That's a huge difference. (Check out Ephesians 2:10.) Others wonder if grace makes us lazy or passive. But real grace isn't soft or passive—it's powerful. It changes everything from the inside out. It's what regenerates your heart, helps you grow, and gives you strength to keep going when you feel done. (See Titus 2:11–12.)

And yes, sometimes grace can feel unfair. How can God just *forgive*? But grace isn't about ignoring justice—it's about Jesus taking justice on Himself so we could receive mercy. At the cross, God didn't choose one or the other. He brought justice *and* mercy together (Romans 3:25–26).

Sola Gratia vs. the Cultural Narrative

What the world says:

- "I define myself."
- "I earn my worth."
- "I deserve good things."
- "Spirituality should serve my needs."

What grace says:

- "You are lost, but loved."
- "You cannot save yourself—but Jesus has."
- "You don't deserve grace—and that's why it's beautiful."

What happens when we reject grace?

Pride — We think we did it.

Despair — We fall apart when we fail.

Guilt — We carry shame we were never meant to bear.

A small view of God — He becomes a therapist, not a Savior.

But when we receive grace…
We fall on our knees in awe. And we rise, beloved and secure.

Grace says:

You are not enough.
But Jesus is.
And He gives you everything—freely, fully, forever.

Conclusion

What we've seen:

- *Sola Gratia* means salvation is the unearned, undeserved gift of God's love.
- Scripture anchors it. The Reformers recovered it.
- Only grace can reach dead sinners and raise them to life.
- It stands in direct contrast to today's self-reliant culture.

Why it matters:
Grace is not a soft theological idea. It is the lifeblood of the gospel. If salvation is not *all of grace*, it is not good news at all.

Your invitation:

Marvel at the grace that sought you. Rest in the grace that holds you. And extend the grace that flows through you.

"By grace you have been saved through faith. And this is not your own doing; it is the gift of God."
— *Ephesians 2:8 (ESV)*

Grace is not a side note.
It is the heart of God—and the fountainhead of salvation.

Next, we turn to *Sola Fide*—Only Faith—and discover how this unmerited grace is received: not by effort, but by resting in Christ alone.

CHAPTER 4: SOLA FIDE – ONLY FAITH

The Heart of the Gospel: Trusting Christ

Think about this: when you step into a hot air balloon, you trust it will lift you. When you drive on a two-way road, you trust the other drivers to stay in their lane—even though you've never met them. We show faith like this every day.

In the same way, trusting God is how we begin to truly know Him. Faith isn't blind—it's choosing to believe that God is who He says He is, that His grace is all we need, and that His promises are real.

Introduction: The Faith That Unites Us to Christ

We live in a world where we're constantly told:
"Do better." "Try harder." "Be enough."

People chase success, beauty, and approval, hoping they'll finally feel at peace. Maybe you've felt that pressure too. Maybe you've asked, *"How can I be good enough?"* or *"How can I know that God accepts me?"*

But the gospel gives us a different answer—one filled with freedom and love:

"Trust Christ."

This is what *Sola Fide* means: **Only Faith**.
You don't need to earn God's love. You can't work your way into heaven. All you need is **faith in Jesus**, who already did everything to save you.

Martin Luther called this truth "the article by which the church stands or falls."
John Calvin said, *"Nothing avails but faith—faith which alone apprehends Christ."*

This chapter is deeply personal. It's not just about what we believe. It's about *how we are saved* and *how we know we are loved by God*.

Michael Horton explains it this way:

"Justification by faith sounds strange—people are not asking how they can be right with God but how they can feel better about themselves. But the gospel is not about inner healing first—it's about being declared righteous in Christ."

Maybe you're reading this and wondering, *"Can this be true for me too?"*
Yes, this is for you. No matter your past, your shame, your doubts—God invites you to rest in Jesus.

In this chapter, we'll explore:

- What Sola Fide really means
- Why the Bible teaches it clearly
- How the Reformers rediscovered it
- And why it still matters today—especially in a world full of pressure and performance

Let's take this journey together.

Defining *Sola Fide*

What "Only Faith" Means

- **Sola** means "alone, or only."
- **Fide** means "faith."

So, *Sola Fide* says we are made right with God—not by trying hard or being perfect—but by **faith alone** in Jesus.

Faith doesn't mean just saying, *"Yes, I agree."*
Faith is trusting Jesus with your whole heart—believing that His life, His death, and His resurrection are **enough** for your salvation.

"Faith is the empty hand that receives a gift."
— John Calvin

It's not about how strong your faith is—it's about how strong *Jesus* is. Even a small, trembling faith can hold onto a great Savior.

The Biblical Foundation

The Bible says this again and again:
We are **justified** (declared righteous) by faith—not by doing good works, following laws, or earning God's favor.

Let these verses speak to your heart:

- **Romans 3:28 (NIV)**

    "For we maintain that a person is justified by faith apart from the works of the law."

- **Ephesians 2:8–9 (NIV)**

    "For it is by grace you have been saved, through faith—and this is not from yourselves, it is the gift of God—not by works, so that no one can boast."

- **Galatians 2:16 (NIV)**

    "Know that a person is not justified by the works of the law, but by faith in Jesus Christ… because by the works of the law no one will be justified."

- **Romans 4:5 (NIV)**

    "However, to the one who does not work but trusts God who justifies the ungodly, their faith is credited as righteousness."

What does this mean for you?
It means you don't have to prove yourself to God. Jesus already did. And through **faith**, you receive what He earned: forgiveness, peace, and eternal life.

Reformation Recovery

As previously explained, during the Middle Ages, many people in the church believed that you had to earn salvation through sacraments, prayers, and good behavior. It was like a heavy burden on their backs.

But then came a breakthrough—a return to the Bible.

- **Martin Luther** was crushed by guilt until he read Romans 1:17:

    "The righteous will live by faith."
    In that moment, he finally felt *free*. Not by working harder—but by trusting Christ.

- **John Calvin** said faith is like "a vessel with nothing in it but need."
    Faith doesn't bring anything to God—just an open heart to receive His gift.

- Reformation confessions like **Augsburg** and **Westminster** boldly declared:

We are justified by faith alone—not by faith plus works.

Even today, scholars remind us why this still matters:

- **N.T. Wright**:

    "Justification by faith stands at the center of the biblical story…"

- **D.A. Carson**:

    "The gospel itself stands or falls with the doctrine of justification by faith alone…"

- **Timothy Keller**:

    "Faith alone… frees us from fear, guilt, and pride."

This is not just theology. This is *freedom for your soul*.

Why *Sola Fide* Matters

Theological Necessity

- **Christ's work is enough** – You don't need to add to it.
- **Righteousness is a gift** – Not something you achieve.
- **Faith brings assurance** – You can *know* you're saved because God promised.

Practical Effects

- **Assurance** – You don't have to wonder if you've done "enough." Jesus did it all.
- **Humility** – You can't boast, because it's all grace.
- **Worship** – You'll want to praise God for His kindness.

- **Obedience** – True faith will lead to good works—not to *earn* salvation, but to say *thank you*.

Clarifying Misunderstandings

- *Sola Fide* is **not** against good works.

    "We are created in Christ Jesus to do good works." — *Ephesians 2:10*
    But those works *come after* faith—not before it.

- Sola Fide is **not** lawlessness.
    Faith leads to holy living—not because we *have to*, but because we *want to*.

- Sola Fide is **not** isolation.
    Faith grows best in community—through the church, prayer, and God's Word.

Sola Fide vs. the Modern Narrative

Let's be honest—today's world says the opposite of Only Faith:

"I define my own truth."
"I earn my worth."
"I follow my heart."
"Faith is whatever makes you feel better."

But the gospel says:

"Your worth is given, not earned."
"Truth is a Person—Jesus."
"You don't have to carry the weight. Jesus already did."
"Faith is not about feelings—it's about trust."

Without faith in Christ, we're stuck:

- **Insecurity** – *Have I done enough?*

- **Legalism** – *God only loves me when I'm good or attain something higher through actions or emotional exuberance.*
- **License** – *It doesn't matter what I do.*
- **Despair** – *I'll never be enough.*

But with faith in Christ, we are *free*:

"There is therefore now no condemnation to them which are in Christ Jesus…"
— *Romans 8:1 (KJV)*

As **John Piper** writes:

"When justification by faith grips a soul, it doesn't produce passivity—it creates peace and power at the same time."

Think About It

We've seen that:

- *Sola Fide* means we are justified by faith alone.
- The Bible teaches it clearly.
- The Reformers rediscovered it with joy.
- We still need it today—because the world tells us to perform, but Jesus says, *"Come to Me."*

"For we walk by faith, not by sight."
— *2 Corinthians 5:7 (ESV)*

"I have been crucified with Christ… the life I now live… I live by faith in the Son of God, who loved me and gave himself for me."
— *Galatians 2:20 (ESV)*

Friend, here is your invitation:

- **Rest** – Stop striving. Jesus is enough.
- **Rejoice** – Let worship rise from your heart.
- **Proclaim** – Share this gift of faith with others.

God is not waiting for you to fix yourself.
He is inviting you to trust Him—to lay down your burdens and believe the good news:

"Even the righteousness of God which is by faith of Jesus Christ unto all and upon all them that believe…"
— *Romans 3:22 (KJV)*

You don't have to be enough.
Jesus is.
And by faith, **He is yours.**

CHAPTER 5: SOLI DEO GLORIA – ONLY TO THE GLORY OF GOD

"All of Life, All for God"

The Bible says, "So, whether you eat or drink, or whatever you do, do all to the glory of God." Does that mean even when I'm riding a bicycle?

Introduction: We Were Made to Reflect His Glory

This phrase **Soli Deo Gloria** means – *Only to the glory of God*

But, let's be honest—this can be a hard thing to understand. Not just to explain to others, but even to get clear in your own heart.

Part of the problem? The world has distorted the meaning of glory.

We're taught to chase it everywhere:
- In sports
- In fame and followers
- In money and success
- In power and politics
- Even in church platforms and "spiritual celebrity" vibes

Glory becomes about being seen. Being praised. Being enough.

No wonder it feels confusing.

But the glory of God?
It's not like the spotlight the world runs after.
It's not loud or self-centered.

It's deeper. Truer. And honestly, way more beautiful.

The more you start to see it, the more your view of *everything* begins to shift.

And way more freeing.

But the Christian life offers something better—a deeper purpose.

So, let's dig into the meaning of ***Soli Deo Gloria***: *"To God alone be the glory."* This short phrase speaks to the **whole purpose of your life**—why you were created, why you are saved, and how you live each day. Everything starts with God, flows through God, and returns to God.

A ***think deep*** theologian named Herman Bavinck says:

"The chief purpose of creation and redemption is the manifestation of God's glory."

God didn't make us to impress Him. He made us so that, by knowing Him, we could reflect His beauty to the world. The Christian life is not about **proving** ourselves to God—it's about **responding** to His sovereignty and love.

What Does Soli Deo Gloria Mean?

Let's break it down simply:

- **Soli** – "Alone" or "Only"
- **Deo** – "To God"
- **Gloria** – "Glory," "Honor," or "Praise"

So together, it means: **To God alone be all the glory.**

Every part of life—your work, your talents, your struggles, your joy—can reflect how amazing and good God is. And this truth connects everything else we believe. Only Scripture, Only Faith, Only Grace, and Only Christ—all of it points back to this: **God deserves the glory**

What Is Soli Deo Gloria and Why Does It Matter?

1. Defining the Phrase

Let's start at the root. *Soli Deo Gloria* is Latin for **To God alone be the glory**.

- **Soli** = Alone
- **Deo** = To God
- **Gloria** = Glory or Praise

This phrase is more than fancy theology—it's the core of everything. It says: *God is the source, the reason, and the goal.* The glory doesn't go to humanity, culture, religion, or creation. It goes back to God. Always. Every time.

"So, whether you eat or drink, or whatever you do, do all to the glory of God." — *1 Corinthians 10:31 (ESV)*

2. Because of Who God Is

We don't glorify God just because it sounds spiritual. We glorify Him because of who He **is**.

God is holy. God is eternal. God is powerful, sovereign, wise, good, and full of unconditional love.

"Worthy are you, our Lord and God, to receive glory and honor and power, for you created all things, and by your will they existed and were created." — *Revelation 4:11 (ESV)*

His nature doesn't need our applause. It demands our response. He isn't like us—He's the one everything depends on. Unlike postmodern ideas that say truth is subjective and each person creates their own meaning, *Soli Deo Gloria* says: *God is ultimate meaning. He's not found—He reveals.*

3. God's Design for Humanity

Here's a truth we forget: you were created for glory. Not to *receive* it. But to *reflect* it.

"…everyone who is called by my name, whom I created for my glory, whom I formed and made." — *Isaiah 43:7 (ESV)*

From the start, God designed us to be mirrors of His truth—images of His character. The goal was never to build a brand around ourselves or hustle to become "somebody." Our calling is to show *His* greatness in everyday life.

John Calvin said it this way:

"Man's chief end is to glorify God and to enjoy Him forever."

You don't need the spotlight. You carry it.

4. Salvation Magnifies Glory

When God saves us, it's not just a rescue mission—it's a glory story.

"For from him and through him and to him are all things. To him be glory forever. Amen." — *Romans 11:36 (ESV)*

Redemption wasn't plan B. Grace wasn't a backup idea. From creation to the cross, God was revealing His glory. Every act of mercy, every moment of love, every drop of blood—it all pointed back to His power and compassion.

Unlike self-help movements or spiritual performance models that say "fix yourself," the gospel says "God did the work—receive it."

5. A Correction to Self-Glory

Let's be honest—our hearts love being the center. Our generation grew up hearing "be your own truth," "follow your heart," and "make your own greatness." But Scripture flips that narrative.

"They did not honor him as God... but exchanged the glory of the immortal God for images..." — *Romans 1:21–23 (ESV)*

Soli Deo Gloria says: *Stop the hustle.* We weren't made for self-glory. That road leads to pride and exhaustion—or insecurity and fear. This isn't about performing. It's about redirecting. You don't have to shine to impress God. Just point your light toward Him.

6. Reformation Rediscovery

During the Reformation, a group of believers rose up to say: **"It's all God."** Martin Luther, John Calvin, and others took Scripture seriously—and they found freedom.

The Belgic Confession (1561) declared:

"To Him alone we must be subject, and to Him is all glory due."

They realized: salvation is not a scoreboard. God doesn't grade us. He invites us. We're not performing. We're responding.

The Reformers weren't trying to add pressure. They were trying to remove it.

How Do We Live to the Glory of God?

1. Faith That Trusts

Previously, we talked about faith as being one of the "Onlys", but it is also a way of giving glory to God.

Let's clear the air: Faith is not performance. It's not a way to earn points with God. It's not just about checking spiritual boxes or doing things to make ourselves feel more "Christian."

Faith is about believing and trusting God.

Not just believing *in* Him, but believing *Him*. His character. His promises. His Word. It's trusting that when He speaks, it's true—even when it's hard to see.

"Now faith is the assurance of things hoped for, the conviction of things not seen." — *Hebrews 11:1 (ESV)*

"Without faith it is impossible to please him, for whoever would draw near to God must believe that he exists and that he rewards those who seek him." — *Hebrews 11:6 (ESV)*

Faith says:

- "God, I take you at your Word."
- "You said you love me. I believe it."
- "You said you finished the work. I'll stop trying to finish what You already completed."

It's not self-help. It's **God-help**.

Unlike the messages of Deconstructionism, which teach us to doubt everything, or New Age spirituality, which tells us truth is relative and changeable, Scripture calls us to anchor ourselves in the **unchanging God**. Faith isn't vague energy or wishful thinking—it's **confidence in the real, personal, active God** who has revealed Himself.

And it's restful.

"For we who have believed enter that rest…" — *Hebrews 4:3 (ESV)* "Anyone who enters God's rest also rests from his works, just as God did from His." — *Hebrews 4:10 (ESV)*

Faith stops the spinning wheels of "Am I enough?" and replaces them with "God is enough."

This is what Abraham did. He didn't build altars to prove himself. He trusted.

"No distrust made him waver concerning the promise of God, but he grew strong in his faith as he gave glory to God." — *Romans 4:20 (ESV)*

In believing, he glorified God. No act of obedience shines brighter than simple, humble trust.

So if you feel tired from trying to "do better," pause. God's not waiting for you to impress Him. He's asking you to believe Him.

Because **faith isn't about doing more**. It's about **trusting the One who already did enough**.

Now, here's the top secret that isn't a secret. It's three connected words that are at the core. **FAITH — BELIEF — TRUST**.

They mean believing God and putting your trust in Him, no matter what. They mean resting in Him and experiencing the peace that naturally follows. This is the essence of glorifying God.

Abraham believed God and gave God the glory, and that's what all those great people in the Bible did. It means believing in Him for salvation and trusting Him in every moment and circumstance thereafter.

In the book of Revelation Jesus asks if he will find faith when he returns. It seems the world will be putting its trust in other things, rather than in a trustworthy God.

Trust God, and that gives him glory.

2. Everyday Life as Sacred

Yes—your regular, normal life matters. Your job. Your studies. Making toast. Sending emails. Raising kids. Running errands.

Let's repeat it to make the point: "So, whether you eat or drink, or **whatever you do, do all to the glory of God.**" — *1 Corinthians 10:31 (ESV)*

Martin Luther once wrote:

"God Himself is milking the cows through the vocation of the milkmaid."

Translation? God works through us—even in the most ordinary things. You don't need a platform or pulpit. Your life, lived in dependence, glorifies God.

3. Guided by Scripture, Empowered by the Spirit

We're not just floating through life hoping to make good choices. God actually guides us—through His Word and Spirit.

"Whatever you do… do everything in the name of the Lord Jesus…" — *Colossians 3:17 (ESV)*

"It is God who works in you to will and to act in order to fulfill His good purpose." — *Philippians 2:13 (ESV)*

God isn't a distant observer—He's right here, working through us. And our response to His love shows up in real ways: Forgiveness when we've been hurt. Kindness when it's inconvenient. Generosity when no one's watching. Truth spoken even when it's hard.

These responses say, "God, I trust You. I live for You."

4. A Truth to Proclaim

Truth matters. And not just private truth—the gospel is for everyone.

"Then you will know the truth, and the truth will set you free." — *John 8:32 (ESV)*

"I am not ashamed of the gospel, for it is the power of God for salvation..." — *Romans 1:16 (ESV)*

We don't share the message because we feel guilty if we don't. We share it because people need it. This is the kind of truth that breaks chains and heals hearts. It's not about arguments—it's about freedom. Real freedom. It's about sharing God's compassion. And by sharing this good news, we give glory to God.

As C.H. Spurgeon, a super-brain Christian influencer from the 1800s, whose books are still popular today, said:

"The gospel is like a lion. You don't have to defend it. Just let it loose."

5. Rest That Reveals Trust

Rest is holy. Jesus rested. God rested. We're allowed to breathe.

"Come to me, all who labor and are heavy laden, and I will give you rest." — *Matthew 11:28 (ESV)*

This is a Sabbath rest seven days a week. Whether active or relaxing, God's rest comes from experiencing the peace He gives. When we do that, we stop pretending we're in control—and start believing He really is. That is a recognition of **To God alone be the glory.**

Conclusion: A Life That Points to God

Soli Deo Gloria isn't just theology—it's lifestyle. It's how we work. Rest. Pray. Create. Play. Speak. Love.

"To Him be glory in the church and in Christ Jesus throughout all generations, forever and ever. Amen." — *Ephesians 3:21 (ESV)*

It means:

- Trusting God's wisdom and strength
- Letting grace shape your decisions
- Speaking truth boldly
- Living free, because Jesus already did the hard part

Finally, can we give God glory even when riding a bicycle? The answer is, Yes!

This is not pressure. It's joy. It's FREEDOM. All of life. All for God.

Soli Deo Gloria.

FINALLY: ANCHORED IN THE FIVE SOLAS FOR OUR AGE

"You Are Loved. You Are Held. You Have a Purpose."

We live in a loud, fast, and often confusing world. Opinions change every day. Social media tells us who to be. The news brings fear. Even our hearts sometimes feel unsure. But in the middle of this storm, God gives us something firm—something unshakable.

He gives us **the gospel**, and at the center of the gospel are **five clear truths**—the Five Solas, a **survival guide** for life.

Only Christ

Jesus says He is the door and **the key** to an eternal relationship with God.

Jesus is a full member of the triune God. You can't upgrade or downgrade him with addons. He is the way, the truth, and the life. No one comes to the Father but through Him.

And He loves you, and will never leave you or forsake you.

Only Scripture

The world has a thousand voices. But the Word of God is one voice—**true, clear, and loving**.

When life gets confusing, when doubts whisper in your mind, when culture tells you lies—come back to Scripture. It doesn't just give advice. It gives life. Let the Bible be your compass when you feel lost, your food when you feel weak, your flashlight in the dark.

Scripture is **your GPS**

Only Grace

The world says, "Work harder. Be better. Earn your worth." But God says, "My child, I love you. Let me save you."

With grace, you don't have to climb your way to heaven. God came down to lift you up. You don't need to prove yourself. You are **already loved**. God's grace doesn't run out. It flows like a river—strong enough for your deepest sin, soft enough for your most tender tears.

Grace is a **free gift** from God. Eternal life. That's right, free, unconditional, and unmerited favor.

Only Faith.

God is not waiting for you to fix yourself. He is inviting you to trust Him—to lay down your burdens and believe the good news. Faith doesn't mean "just believe hard enough." It means: *"I trust Jesus with all that I am."*

Even when your faith feels weak, Jesus holds you strong. You don't have to fix yourself before coming to Him. **Come as you are.** Let go of fear. Trust in the One who has already finished the work.

If you were to get into a **hot air balloon**, a parachute, or an airplane, you would put your trust in physical dynamics and the competency of engineers who made these devices.

Even more, you can trust in the maker of this world. You can believe that He gave His life so that you might live. You can trust Him through every trial, through every moment of your life.

Because He is trustworthy.

The glory of God alone

God is the Alpha and Omega, the beginning and the end. He is the creator of this magnificent universe, and the one who showed Himself and paid the penalty for our sins.

God the Father, God the Son. God, the Holy Spirit.

Three in One. Magnificent.

Worthy of Glory.

Soli Deo Gloria isn't just theology—it's lifestyle. It's how we work. Rest. Pray. Create. Speak. Love. God is worthy, and trusting Him means complete dependence on Him, and that is the highest recognition of His glory.

We live in that trust when we eat and drink, whether **in everything, and even when doing everyday tasks like riding a bicycle**.

To Him be the Glory..

Why the Five Solas Still Matter—for *You*

These are not just old ideas. They are **anchors**. They are not just for pastors or theologians. They are **for you**. Right here. Right now.

You were made for these truths—and they were given in love, to hold your heart forever.

These truths are not just about church history—they are about your story:

- In your friendships
- In your struggles
- In your classes and jobs
- In your quiet time and in your darkest night
- In your joy and in your sin
- In your search for meaning and hope

Let them whisper to your heart:

"Since the solas are true to Scripture, all Christians in every generation ought to remember, embrace, and proclaim them." — Stephen J. Wellum

---

Here are a few ways that they apply. There are many more:

1. Secured in God's Unfailing Love

"For I am sure that… nothing… will be able to separate us from the love of God in Christ Jesus our Lord." — *Romans 8:38–39 (ESV)*

Even when you fall—God still loves you.
Even when you feel alone—He is near.
Even when your world shakes—Jesus holds you.

---

2. Held by Abundant Grace

"But God, being rich in mercy… made us alive together with Christ." — *Ephesians 2:4–5 (ESV)*

You are not too far gone. You are not too messy.
God's mercy is **richer than your mistakes.**
His love made you alive—and that love will never let go.

---

3. Never Alone: His Perpetual Presence

"God is our refuge and strength, a very present help in trouble." — *Psalm 46:1 (ESV)*
"I will never leave you nor forsake you." — *Hebrews 13:5 (ESV)*

There will be hard days. There will be nights when you cry alone. But hear this:
You are never truly alone.
The God who made the stars is the same God who holds your heart.

A Final Charge

Don't leave the Five Solas on a shelf.
Don't keep them as facts in your head.
Let them sink deep into your heart. Let them shape the way you love, live, suffer, and dream.

And remember:

- Only Christ is your anchor.
- Only Scripture is your light.
- Only Grace is your freedom.
- Faith alone is your lifeline.
- The glory of God alone is your purpose.

These truths won't just change what you know.
They will **transform who you are.**

"He alone is my rock and my salvation, my fortress; I shall not be shaken." — *Psalm 62:6 (ESV)*

You are loved.
You are seen.
You are chosen.
You are held.
You are free.

***Soli Deo Gloria.* Forever.**

www.ingramcontent.com/pod-product-compliance
Lightning Source LLC
Chambersburg PA
CBHW052126070526
44586CB00016B/2100